Denouement ... an unravelling

Khushnam Wadia - Engineer

BookLeaf Publishing

India | USA | UK

Presentation by *BookLeaf Publishing*

Web: www.bookleafpub.com

E-mail: info@bookleafpub.com

ISBN: 9789360949471

First edition 2024

DEDICATION

This collection of poems is dedicated to
Hormosd and Farzad ...

my raisons d'etre and the
much-needed impetus to continue the process
of unravelling

ACKNOWLEDGEMENT

This book today sees the light of day because of two people who have always supported my writing and encouraged me to publish over many, many years. My sister Armin, who would save the scraps of paper on which I would write my poetry growing up, for believing that it was something worth sharing with the world. And my husband Hormosd, who has been ever so loving and encouraging and supportive of my writing forays since the time we met and like Armin in the early years, has always been a vocal advocate for me to publish.

I thank my parents, Rohinton and Jasmine for their love and support always, for celebrating my successes to this day, no matter how small, and for being there at every step of the journey.

I also want to thank Hiraji, Nergish, Aloo, Mahiar, Khurshid, Mahtab, Delnaz and Hormazd, and later Dilnavaz, Kersy and Danesh, who have been such an integral part of my journey growing up, along with my parents and sister, and without whose presence I would not be the person I am today.

A big shout out to Farzad, who is my raison d'etre, my compass. My humble gratitude to Farzad along with Naisha, Vaspaan, Farhan and Nasha for bringing the joy that some would say was lost and for being the everlasting hope that Life has to offer.

I would like to acknowledge my gratitude to those without whom *untying* would have been most difficult, my mentors, guides and the ones who continue to show me the Path, Gargi Lakhani and Farrokh Buchia.

Most importantly my complete gratitude to the Divine, for His Grace and Love, that has always been there, especially on the darkest of days when I could not feel it.

PREFACE

Denouement is a collection of poems that I have written over a long period of time. Writing poetry has always been something that, for me, has flowed at will and not something that I have been able to summon up as and when needed.

These poems have been written at different points in my life, in times of great trial as also in times of great joy and as such reflect my being in that moment.

No matter the highs and lows, the process of unravelling into mySelf has been one of utmost joy and replete with rewards and I would not have it any other way. I only have compassion for this process of Be(com)ing human in all its complexities and at the heart of it am in love with all of its simplicity.

Alone!

Alone

I stand

staring into the world

there is

your world and my world.

Each hold the other

In its wrathful care

You in your world and me in mine

We together, stand alone and stare.

My world is about the pain,

The excruciating pain

That I feel when I see,

Your world, not recognising me.

To you, I'm a lump

Heavy and bogged down, like a stone

Which makes you sink

As if you were tied to one.

Lend a Hand

3

Give the world a penny

Give the world a smile

Lend a hand happily

Lend yourself for a while.

Feel the pain you can't see

Let yourself flow and be

Let the tear roll down the eye

The one that has been but cannot be.

It hurts to hold it within

Packed and pressurized to its brim

I can't feel it but I know it's there

So can you feel for me, can you help me bear.

Asking for Alms

My world on my hips

I beg to the world

to help me feed the third one's lips

the little one who within me enfolds

Hand outstretched, I to thee beseech

I thank God for his many seeds

That He planted within me ever so lovingly

Leaving me to look after its myriad needs.

Furry

5

When someone goes away

Someone you adore

Someone who's by your side stayed

You're going to miss them so much more.

Why did you have to go away

Why couldn't by my side you stay

I wanted you to be my friend

Forever till the end.

I'm sad and low

I'm angry

God had to make you go

I only want to say to Him

'I'M ANGRY, IT'S UNFAIR, IT STINKS!!!'

6

Wherever you are,

I hope you're safe and happy

You'll be missed and loved forever

Oh I wish that I could rub your belly

Just once more!

Aeons

I know not why,

I know not how,

I fell in love with you

I don't understand now

I feel the pain

The uttered refrain

Of trust lost and found

In deep realms that astound

A time long gone

An era that has passed

Surges forth with emotions

Earlier left unexplained

The mortal body

Houses the immortal soul

Bringing forth the pain

And numerous stories untold

Of the times, cycles ago

When light we see left the star high above

Of princes and princesses

Of injustices done

This life and the next

The pain gets passed through

Your soul is the same

Although the body that houses it is new

Pass through my body

Renew my energy

Let me flow and enfold

In your arms Mother Earth

Help me touch the seed within

Help me see the Divine

That's part of me and has always been

There, To light up the path

I will not let myself feel!

My hands folded tight

My posture upright

My legs squeezed and folded

With my own self I fight

I will not let myself feel

The iron bars to my heart are sealed

I'll scream till my voice grows hoarse

Oh! I will not let myself feel

You will never know the pain within

Why just you? I won't even let myself in

For I fear what I will find there

Imagining what I can't bear, I cringe.

Armoured

Numb as the flesh immersed in ice

Burnt as dry skin in the sun

The heart can't see..

The stomach can't feel

I need to get the scales up...

Toughen up and close down

In case an arrow comes through

There will be no softness left for it to pierce

Mutiny

I see your angry face

Blowing steam in front of me

You put me back in my own place

Mirroring the anger I feel

My scream so silent

It can rip a heart apart

My world so constricting

It makes me choke and gasp.

I flail my hands around

In absolute agony

No matter how hard I try, all I see is me.

Cause it's within that there's the mutiny

Like sinking in a quicksand

Nothing helps pull me out

All around is the cruel world

Mocking my frailty, my pleas, my shouts.

Muddled

Jittery and shaking a lot

My hands do not seem to stop

Knotted and twisted tight

My stomach plummets from a height

No matter what words I say

No matter what I try to argue away

It screams mighty and loud

I can't seem to handle the crowd.

I want to be by myself

No, people, no feelings, no help.

Just calm and conscious, at peace

Understanding, accepting,... relief.

I am angry at several things

Thousands, I don't know what to say

I'm scared that my heart's fluttering

Would muddle the words in my head.

I'm angry at several things

Thousands, I don't know what to say

I'm scared that my heart's fluttering

Would muddle the words in my head.

Messy

The world seems a murmur

A swish a fervor

You show me some faces

And then there's just a blur

What am I supposed to get

What do I discover

In this whole mess

I feel like a blunder

Many a time I wonder

If I'm meant to find out

Many a time I surrender

As I can't find a way out

Many a time I feel

Like in a whirlpool I'm stuck

Drowning, sucked in... I feel fucked up

The worlds, both yours and mine

Feel like such a mess

I can't figure out either

... no success!!

A Four Year Old's Dream

Sitting on hardwood floors

Hands folded tight

I dream a dream many towers high

A four year old's dream amongst the cloudy
skies

Of a heavenly place very far away

Of a palace with lawns and forests

Of a prince kind and generous

Of only Happiness all night and day

I will have whatever I desire

There will be no questions no ire

Fineries like love, will flow

I will have to hurt no more

Away from this lonely large room

Away from these mean people

Away from the lump in my heart

Control

I want to control

The flight of a fly

The wasp's sting

To let me not die

To let you not win

The time of dawn

The coming of spring

When you don't control me

I win, I win

It's about who twitched first

Who let the eye blink

Who gave in to the worst

Who let the nightmare begin

The world I feel, I hold in my grasp

When I hold the strings, the stick, the clamps,

Oh how I'm deluded,

The control eluded

I'm left but grasping at straws

The Witch

Caged in this body

With bars of bone

Burning red hot Cinders

I'm coming undone

Angry mad thoughts are running

coursing through the veins

Waiting to explode out

Grey matter, liquids, entrails.

I don't know how I came to be

Entrapped, locked, squished inside of me

Like Frankenstein centuries ago

There must have been a master putting it all in

Aeons of hatred, anger, revenge

Crazy, screwed up, Kookoo, unhinged

I feel like a mad woman on prowl

Scared but oh so scorned

Hunted by men with wooden clubs & axes

The pounding at the door intensifies

Cornered in a round room with no corners

I sit shivering in the face of death

I quiver, I rant, I plot & I scheme

I have to get out before they get in

With heaven & hearth both closing in

I bite my hand .... and kill

A little blue whisper

She put into a bottle

A little blue whisper

And watches as a wisp of smoke

Glides down the curvature of the bottle

A hundred things to tell has she

But where to start, what to share

Who would the listener be

Will her ancestry he be able to bear

She will tell the tale of her childhood

When innocence was meant to be

But stripped had she been

Of all joy and fantasy

Then the tale that happened centuries ago

When at an empty crib she stared

Pulled from her grasp, made to forgo

Looking at what was to be her little angel's bed

A cork she has put

Shut the bottle down

The whisper gasps for breath

It doesn't want to die now

It wants to speak

It wants to be heard

But who will the listener be

Will he hear what she has to say or deny her
vehemently

Heavy is the head that wears the crown

Heavy is the head that wears the crown

So maybe I should put it down

I may not sit on the throne

But at least I won't feel like a stone

And maybe once again I can move

Let my arms flow around the wind

And move my feet

To a beat that is my own

Joy

Fragrance fills the air

Emanating slowly from the earth below

Its waves, through the nose, hit the brain

And from there through the body it flows

Awakening, with its strength, all the cells

As wave after wave inundate the senses

Oh how could just one sweet fragrance

Work a wonderful magic so dense?

It heralds the burst

From within Mother Earth's bosom

Lush and green life soon it will envelop

And with it, slowly, other colours will come.

She closes her eyes

And spreads out her hands

And in her loving embrace

Awaits the showers, her friends.

The world grows dim

And heaven yields its sword

As the clanging of its cymbals

Signal the start of the downpour.

A huge drop splats

Smacks the forehead red.

And then with its cooling touch

On its slow downward journey it treads.

It inches its way across the cheek

Tickles the neck and slides further

Coming to rest on her cheek

As there it nestles, she lets out a murmur.

A sigh accompanies the arching back

Sensuousness reaches its threshold

A moan mirrors her feelings within

As in her own arms she folds.

The shower takes over

As she is washed in pleasure by batches

As hundreds of drops are now making their way

Until within her the desire finally hatches.

Like the white of a chicken egg

That slips out with ease

She has slipped into this drowsy rest

Feeling happy and pleased.

Laden Grey Sky

She remembers the time he held her hand

And sprayed her with a water hose

She remembers being asked out again and again

Realizing he wouldn't for an answer take a no.

She remembers the day they stood

Before an altar to vow and pray

And then when they held within their arms

God's little angels so tiny and frail.

She remembers the day when these angels had
angels of their own

The day he finally held her hand and spoke

"I'll love you forever and by your side be"

But then… something within her heart broke!

The angels had flown to charter their own course

And then suddenly one day… he too went away

Today she sits kneeling curled up in a ball

Remembering him under the laden sky grey.

The Sun and the Moon

Oh seed, you haven't fallen far from the tree

The very shade you despised, you've grown up
to be

It's dark and dinghy under your care

The leaves do not grow the flowers do not dare

For you are the tree that ruled with an iron fist,

Looking at what nutrients each received

The roots were not yours to control

Nor the fate of those you shaded

They were to grow

No matter how much on them you waited

You waited on them day in and day out

Hoping the sun would notice and the moon's
glow would see

What a good tree you've been

Helping those in need

And yet ...

The sun's been shining all along

The moon's glow waxing and waning yet there

And you've seen

Through the leaves

That shaded their song

My Mirror

Like a mirror, I can't wipe clean

I see you reflect back to me

What I tried to erase years ago

Telling myself, This I cannot be

I cannot be jealous

I cannot be vain

I cannot be mutinous

I mustn't feel disdain

We must be sunshine

The world is happy to see

Smiling, laughing, helping kind

A Pollyanna just doing her duty

Hide the feeling of inadequacy

For if others do it see ... ...

One cannot even imagine ...

Quick! Shake the image ... let it be.

Today,

The facade cracks

The fissures deepen

Out ooze the shadows

So far well hidden

Seeing them in you

Alas! I can no longer them ignore

Slowly and surely as I hold your little hand

Showing me that like the little train, puffing up
the hill

Yes, we can...

We can be jealous

We can be vain

We can be mutinous

and feel disdain

We can be joyous

We can be wild

We can be childlike

Taking in the delights

The world is beautiful

With people of all kind

Thank you for the journey
Back to Wholeness

                    ... my child

SAMARAH

On an expanse of fine brown

A speck appears

Its black robes billowing in the wind

In this large nothingness

Some life has emerged

Like water to the parched earth, it moves.

A lonely figure for miles around

Trudges along an age-old path

She leads to the source of sustenance

That has helped generations grow old and then restart

The oversized robe surges from above her face

It reveals the thin pale lips underneath

The sharp bridge of the nose

Is laden with heirloom nose rings

As she slowly raises her eyes

Her longing pierces the soul

The pain and the tribulations

One knows on her life has taken a toll.

A dark black bead

In her deep blue iris

Like the ocean floor

It holds treasures within.

It's the eyes that steal your breath

Like spears searing through the body,

One can feel her criticism and disdain,

And to add, her raw sensuality;

she's for sure no small lady.

Like a mighty tigress she has fought on,

Like an untiring tortoise she has plodded,

To make this journey without, her journey within

She has had to use her perseverance, down to
her every shred.

Carrying within her bosom the elixir of life

She moves along the deserted Sahara

Feeding it to the courageous and the fearful,

the distressed and the damned

A woman with the heart of lion,

                    The water bearer,

SAMARAH